# ASCENSION

# ASCENSION

for marilyn,
dancing the
dreamtime . . .

peace,

GIOVANNI SINGLETON

giovanni singleton

*Counterpath*
*Denver* 2012

Counterpath
Denver, Colorado
www.counterpathpress.org



Library of Congress Cataloging in Publication Data
singleton, giovanni.
Ascension / giovanni singleton.
p. cm.
ISBN 978-1-933996-26-4 (pbk. : alk. paper)
I. Title.
PS3619.I576A9 2012
811'.6—dc23
2011036476

## ACKNOWLEDGMENTS

My thanks to the editors of the following journals and anthologies where these poems, some in earlier versions, first appeared: *MiPOesias.com* ("DAY 45"); *nocturneseditions.org* ("the odds"); *Fence* and anthologized in *A Best of Fence: The First Nine Years* ("DAY 11"); *Five Fingers Review* issues 18 and 19 (excerpts from "melanin suite"); *VOLT* issue 16 ("DAY 18", "DAY 23", "DAY 39", and "DAY 43"); *Poet Lore* ("DAY 16" and "DAY 37"); and *Writing Self and Community: A Norton Anthology of African American Poetry After the Civil Rights Movement* ("DAY 33", "DAY 36", "DAY 41", and "DAY 48").

Sincere gratitude to: my family and Lucille Clifton, Alice Coltrane, Sarah Coon, Patricia Dienstfrey, Kathy Evans, Amy Ford, Marvin Glass, Dale Going, Anne & Ellis Hamilton,

Lyn Hejinian, David Henderson, Sean Hill, Brenda Hillman, Douglas Kearney, Michelle Bradshaw, Bobbie Lewis, Deborah Lokteff, devorah major, Denise Newman, Douglas "D. Scot" Miller, E. Ethelbert Miller, Harryette Mullen, Napa Valley Writers' Conference, Duriel E. Harris, Dana Teen Lomax, Cave Canem, Carolyn Micklem, Indigo Moor, opalmoore, Julie Ezelle Patton, Marilyn Ringer, gini savage, Regina Schwartz, Evie Shockley, Squaw Valley Community of Writers, Brady Upham, Bonnie V. Winston, Trixie and Percy: The Best Pugs Ever, Gloria Jean Walker, Ronaldo V. Wilson, C. D. Wright, Toni Wynn, and Al Young.

CONTENTS

*for love*

# THE ODDS

read the leaves roll the dice shuffle the cards lay the runes write some poems and pray pray pray
shuffle the cards lay the runes write some poems and pray pray read the leaves roll the dice
shuffle the cards lay the runes write some poems and pray pray read the leaves roll the dice
shuffle the cards lay the runes write some poems and pray pray read the leaves roll the dice
shuffle the cards lay the runes write some poems and pray pray read the leaves roll the dice

# EAR OF THE BEHEARER

*A daybook composed during musician and spiritual leader Alice Coltrane's (Swamini Turiyasangitananda) 49-day transition through the bardo (the intermediate states between death and rebirth).*

{011207.friday}

## DAY 1

feather
rattle

sky  sky

drum
turtle

cry  cry

talking
stick

eye  eye

fire in
the skull

{011307.saturday}

## DAY 2

blues poet stands
at the crossroads framed
in indigo light.

he reaches his hand around
to his left side, slits himself
open as if to gut a fish.

once inside, he feels
his heart, touches
his liver. but he

is not an oyster. he has
not eaten sand. what then
can a pearl be?

{011407.sunday}

DAY 3

a bouquet
of irises

one by one
opens its

eyes a little
each day

determined
to witness

{011507.monday}

## DAY 4

one part spring. one part rain.
one part summer. one part absence.
one part autumn. one part gone.
one part winter. one part parting.

leaves far from gathered.

{011607.tuesday}

## DAY 5

God
where
are you?

the sound
of gravel
underfoot

Where
could
you be?

{011707.wednesday}

DAY 6

first-person narrative:

I AM

NOT FOR SALE

AT ANY PRICE

end of story.

{011807.thursday}

DAY 7

and just what color is blue?

names forgive their meaning
sundays are for what a mind thinks

history of touching
stretches out beneath the surface

the only way to sleep is to
imagine it is raining

and it is
raining

wind blows open and over
a final line of defense

what happens happens
far away

{011907.friday}

## DAY 8

through eyes
slightly opened,
i watch the

slits in the
guest house
blinds

hold vigil for
December sun
to rise

a mask
in search
of a face

today some
things will no
longer be true.

some things
we'll deny
ever knowing.

{012007.saturday}

DAY 9

the sun arrived
early. a radiant
compass

embraced by time,
she walked toward
winter's end

and thus became
her calling—to cry
a litter each day

until all of hers
and the world's
sorrows dissolved.

and the ground
was covered with
a green grass.

{012107.sunday}

## DAY 10

crouching down
in half light,

the wind again
picks up, rushes

forward, hurls
us to next.

we did not know
where we were going.

once, we went
way back to

where every sound
was a story and

every silence
epic.

{012207.monday}

DAY 11

at night
high beams scan the
unseeable distance

an untitled landscape

black is not
a shade but rather
an impression

oil on canvas

•

scratch and sniff lawns
on southern streets where
one sips lemonade or

iced tea before hosing
down weeds in
the way of light.

still life with

•

jars marked and mislabeled for
proper identification
enjambment is a way of doing it.

standing room only

•

drums do not go quietly
their chained rhythm treads
water and stretches of road.

ocean as enclosure.

{012307.tuesday}

## DAY 12

dead fox beside the road. the risk
we all run.

{012407.wednesday}

DAY 13

the readied hook
the swung rod

lowered bait
gets you hooked

pulled up and
into open air.

listen.

let me tell you
where i've been.

before the
tide turns.

{012507.thursday}

## DAY 14

once a year, the villagers
and all the people
within

gather by the river,
push off candle-
lit paper boats

hand-written names
of the Absent their
singular cargo.

{012607.friday}

## DAY 15

they sat for
a time watching
the fire burn

how ghosts climbed
into him through
the palms of

his outstretched
hands

their cattle bore
the cross

made her
"Redeemer."

{012707.saturday}

## DAY 16

every full moon
night for most of
her life

she went to the
stream below
Yellow Mountain

each time
she placed
her cupped
hands into

the water's flow
around the moon's
circumference

hoping to fish
salt

from the sky.

{012807.sunday}

## DAY 17

new to it all
she fell down
to her knees.

new to it all
she stood up
again.

new to it all
she opened
her eyes.

darkness receded
though she could
not see.

god had fallen in.

{012907.monday}

## DAY 18

because he disremembered
the past, the past bound
itself to him.

it creased his mouth.
furrowed his brow.
grayed his hair.

when he spoke, his voice
used the language of
disremembering.

because he disremembered
his ex-wife, their love bound
itself to him.

whenever he turned around,
one could see her face looking
out from the back of his head.

{013007.tuesday}

## DAY 19

silence and darkness
i'm recording you.
just isolated moments

going farther and
farther out

touching what then
for as long as it takes

everything is allowed
or its reflection
treated declaratively.

{013107.wednesday}

DAY 20

through a gate that cast
no shadow steps lead

to a house no
longer standing

inside, each room
had become another

what was ready-made
and monstrous

someone else drew
the picture

entered antlers first

{020107.thursday}

## DAY 21

she went up
the main road
a ways

*she did*
*she did*

a button fell
from her one
good dress

sweat rolled
slowly down
her brow

*it did*
*it did*

she looked
and looked
all around

*she did*
*she did*

but she never
she never
came back

{020207.friday}

## DAY 22

*paintbrushes, buttercups, hemlock*

purple lupine make little beans
after their flowers are gone

three dogs, two men, three women
eucalyptus trees whose leaves
fell quite some time ago.

*chamomile, forget-me-nots, sage*

mallow shoots itself up and
branches into trees.

we don't step on the black scarab
beetle in the middle of the path nor
the lizard in sphinx pose.

anthill, gopher hole, hornet's nest.

we see fennel, some non-native thistle.
we eat mustard flowers, taste of Dijon.

*queen anne's lace, nettle, minor's ladder*

and toward the end,
there's a little
climb.

{020307.saturday}

# DAY 23

Too much pruning brings misfortune.

{020407.sunday}

## DAY 24

to confess one

dreams about
manhole covers

another about
elevator shafts

feelings, systems of
belief stored in boxes

a mask searches
for a face

a flickering light
fashions arms

into wings.

{020507.monday}

DAY 25

the circles she spins
widen and emptiness
pours in.

the net catches its prey.

she swallows hard
what love
there is.

{020607.tuesday}

## DAY 26

she pulled the
fish hooks
from his throat

what they could
not extinguish lay
claim to their souls.

he used his eyes
to make waves,
precious gems

{020707.wednesday}

## DAY 27

all that day
labored breath

the dead brushed
against me

a litany of faces
their names beside

Sojourner Truth  Harriet Tubman  Toni Cade Bambara
Mahalia Jackson  Shirley Ann Hemphill  Isabel Sanford
Shirley Chisholm  Clara Ward  Nell Carter  Lynne Thigpen

fantastic gyre
hours struck

memory turned
upon itself

unable to hault
liberation

the soul's cast iron
clapper

{020807.thursday}

DAY 28

## 37. CHIA JÊN

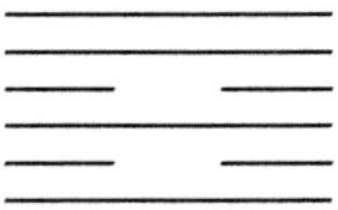

*Write What You Know*

to make chai:

boil water. crush cardamom
and whole black pepper using
mortar and pestle. add

mixture to boiling water.
add whole milk with cream
on top. boil.

add loose black tea. stir.
sugar optional. continue
boiling for a time

before reducing
heat. let sit to
cool.

{020907.friday}

DAY 29

## 37. CHIA JÊN

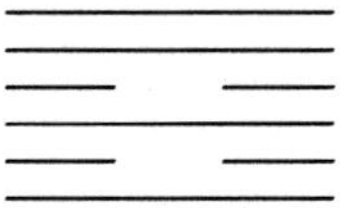

*Write What You Know*, Cont.

Flattery is a fool's delight.

{021007.saturday}

DAY 30

in the Spring
garden, Bessie
the outdoor
cat claws
at her make-
believe mouse.

now is
not the
day for
growing figs.

{021107.sunday}

DAY 31

gold flecked dreams
and footnotes

what to build
the house out of

all ceaselessly
walk around the maximum

redress the broken dish
keep struggling and the fence

{021207.monday}

## DAY 32

by the sounds of it
speech was more than
crossing a river

no telling how
anyone will
come back

goats graze behind
electrified wire

mind moves in
figure eights

all beginnings come
back around and
gather at the end

{021307.tuesday}

## DAY 33

the water by
itself at first.

{seawork}

a black pomfret washed
ashore. its scaled flesh
flapping against the rocks.

a door off its hinges.

why she often kept
the red kettle brewing.

{021407.wednesday}

## DAY 34

in the distance
a woman hears
a train that
isn't there

nevertheless, its
passengers and their
baggage get to where
they're going.

## DAY 35

When I was nine years old,
  I killed a bird; he said.

*Why*? I asked.
Because I wanted to, to
  see what was inside.

*And did you see?*
I don't remember.

*Well then close your eyes.*
Why? he asked.

*To see what's inside*, I said.

{021607.friday}

## DAY 36

we are busy and wanting
to push through light

the bowl i drink from
says we humans keep

cutting back the trees
so that we alone can live

and i realize too just how
much i don't want to be lost

{021707.saturday}

## DAY 37

gusting wind
a fine drizzle

as we come
and go

afraid still of
entering places

from which there
is no returning

i am again
on my knees.

{021807.sunday}

## DAY 38

night descends

fingers a
fine melody

for two

who each
in turn

drop oars
in water

row beyond

light &
shadow

{021907.monday}

DAY 39

*black girl.* u a blk gurl. *black girl.* play on blacktop. play. *girl. black.* u a blk gurl. jump down. turn around. *black girl.* sing. pretty. song. u a blk gurl. *play on.* merry-go-round. you. *black girl.* look. merry-go-mad. you. *black*. you. *girl.*

{022007.tuesday}

DAY 40

gates open as Acknowledgment

deep breath as Psalm

not so much the aspiration as the Pursuance as

the Pronouncement as Resolution as

prayer

sutured under
tongue

{022107.wednesday}

## DAY 41

in a place beyond
sleep i was on the
ground in

the center of a
circle formed by
half-naked people

their faces covered
with brightly
painted masks

horns curved out
from the tops
of their heads

cowbells hung
from collars
around their necks

and cowbells too
where their hands
should've been.

{022207.thursday}

## DAY 42

in a fitful state,
a neighbor swallowed
the moon

people often wish
to receive more
than they give

pronounced the doctor
who weeks earlier had
devoured three planets

{022307.friday}

## DAY 43

i opened my eyes. i did. i found myself inside a watermelon. no remnants of red flesh or black seeds. it was cold and damp in spite of my off-white cable-knit sweater, hat, and wool bell-bottom pants. the vessel, boat or ark, rocked slightly from side to side as i tried to escape. upon standing, however, i realized that i was only six inches tall. i of course shouted for help. a pair of large hands appeared and placed two wooden spoons on either side for oars.

{022407.saturday}

## DAY 44

a mother agrees
to look away

while her son tosses
a coin into the fountain

*did you throw it in yet?*
she asks impatiently.

water roars from
the lion's mouth

*yeh. I been done dat.*
the boy says.

having wished some
odd dream into being.

{022507.sunday}

DAY 45

e World Is Round The World Is Round The World Is Round The World Is Round The World Is Round The Worl

d Is Round The World Is Round The World Is Round The World Is Round The World Is R

The World Is Round The World Is Round The World Is Round The World Is Round The World Is Round

The World Is Round The World Is Round The World Is Round The World Is Round

The World Is Round The World Is Round The World Is Round

, Ain't it

ound The World Is Round The World Is Round The World Is Round The World Is Round The World Is Round Th

{022607.monday}

## DAY 46

a pair of monarch butterflies
their orange and black dimmed
by transcontinental dust

land on the path
just ahead of me

when not in flight, they
continue to move their
wings. considered measure.

an earthly view from which
to catch the wind

{022707.tuesday}

## DAY 47

brown bark stems
picked for pretty

bent forward bodies
tuffs of white

floral arranged in
12-foot window

not meant to frame
now absent master

save the boll weevil
in turns of earth

the unmercied blink
cotton ball eyes

their mournful songs
my own pricked fingers

{022807.wednesday}

DAY 48

elders on their bench upright
and knowing. such and so.

for what would they trade
the solid whites of their eyes?

a right turn. patience nests
in the mind.

salvationers, dark pupils
point themselves into angels.

{030107.thursday}

DAY 49

*go. go. go into*
*the forest.*

*walk among*
*the deer.*

# EXODUS

name giovanni singleton

date 30 june /friday

exodus

(for the blue people, being so)

all night about, above
i go down
stare out at
rushing water
through open
window.

ocean of starlit sky
fills my head
unburdens the weight
of my brain

blooms a lotus flower
its stem stretches up
through the soles of
my feet.

pathway to the country
inside me, its people
seekers naked in the
smokeless clearing.

stained glass maze.
past lifetimes spent
hunting crow.

here they go
here they go
here they go

astral stream of
inky wings
fluttering skyward

echoes of ancient chants
rise from the wooden cage
in my throat.

we are not this
dance but that one.

ط
و
ح
ل
ت
ز
س
ص
ظ
ث
ر
م

name giovanni singleton

date 30 june /friday

exodus cont.

weather flashes across
the backsides of my
eyelids

we me and t. monk too

fold up our chairs, go
inside our cranial houses.

this earthen soul, a flock
of birds

where we are new
      we are new
we are new to this body.

# MELANIN SUITE

1st movement: *burnt umber*

silence.    a guard rail.    teeth knitted together.    a corrugated tongue.

silence    leaves a strain of being work.

of looking

almost        dead.

shade    burns as if to interfere. photographs.    a need to hold

still    for a    moment.        everything that counts        appears

in past tense.        time

accumulates

as in a reflecting pool.

## 2nd movement: *dark brown*

sitting in a darkened hallway.
salt water bodies rock
steady. muffled pounding. door
of no return. closed and
closer. under measured
reconstruction. living seeps
through in echoes. stillness
outside in. a collective breath
persists without
apology. mud-stained spoons
undulate from shore to
distant shore. then one day
walk as if
                    rowing a boat.

3rd movement: *sepia*

anyone configures everyone at random. long and short tangents of breath shift then evaporate. separation from self. remembering and forgetfulness. therein is some predestination. to go on and on and into other structures. a rear exit. the route made visible. singularity of purpose breaks down momentum. sleep moves without sound as in amazing grace.

4th movement: *bronze*

mythical weave of bowed heads.

discontinuous     dreams     and drafts.

drawing hands.

spinning wheel fortune.     stagger the root.

warrior

rifts.     a cataclysmic sight.

acoustic bass.     plucked upright.     all-night

mercurial conjure.     strings.     such tongues ever

leaning as in revelation.

5th movement: *sienna*

we us and thou. voices. sound a downtown destination. the boulevard.
horns blow. fast and furious. ghostly drummer makes flight. some rap

*tap*          *tap*          *tap*          *tap*

conductor of multi-directional speaking. crowds stand behind cranial
walls. all smoke-filled. boy/man. a vast expanse. skeletal remains

spread down on the ground as in quilted covering.

6th movement: *copper*

before beginning          a pause
the sea holds its breath between waves

clapping of wings and of hands penetrate memory
as broken tongues consume open spaces

from whom      from what      do we hide?

fragments take their revenge as in
a jar containing old things

## 7th movement: *russet*

winter morning cracks and peels. exposed brick.

vibrations. dirt comes out.

crushed to the ground. land for invention.

the world lit up from the cold.

itinerant rain gradually falls. a valley of visions.

palms pressed together.

a cross-country train ride as in dreaming.

8th movement: *mahogany*

ecstatic song. <escuchar> a mask in
every note. feather fletched arrows due east.
<las palabras> a ceremonial gesture. premonitions
at the landscape's edge. palatial bed of wildflowers.
<los ojos>  an arc of rainbow light. <la puerta>
ears opening. a refrain as in holy ghosts.

9th movement: *brown*

clouds drift in and out of

parentheses. tightrope miles

    above flickering light.

the slightest distance shifts

whatever is living. a storyteller's

    handiwork. excavated

hieroglyphs. trace back non-linear.

portal to now and anymore. water

    running haloed

songbook. eagle and crow turn around.

fly home. earth free. wings beating as

in a mirror's refrain.

vedAntic

temple prayers

tamborInes and

hallelujah Claps for

Krishna, GanEsha, Shiva

Turiya's sCripture a

jOurney in Satchidananda

beLoved John's

sTained glass face

chuRched in

gospel hArp lord of lords

Detroit miNistry pours from

wami's WurlitzEr

# EYE OF THE BE/HOLDER

I

i

**giovanni singleton** is a poet, teacher, and founding editor of *nocturnes (re)view of the literary arts*, a journal dedicated to the work of artists and writers of the African Diaspora and other contested spaces. A recipient of a New Langton Bay Area Award Show for Literature, she frequently presents on writing, editing, and graphic design at schools and conferences, including the American Literature Association and Spelman College. She has been a fellow at the Squaw Valley Community of Writers, Cave Canem, and the Napa Valley Writers Conference. Her work has appeared on the building of Yerba Buena Center for the Arts and in *Zen Monster, VOLT, Callaloo, Poet Lore, Angles of Ascent: A Norton Anthology, What I Say: Innovative Poetry by Black Writers in America, Kindergarde: Avant-Garde Poems, Plays, & Stories for Children*, and *I'll Drown My Book: A Collection of Conceptual Writing*. singleton has taught at Saint Mary's College, Naropa University, and in museums and schools throughout the San Francisco Bay area.